THE
RESPONSIBILITY
OF THE
CHRISTIAN MUSICIAN

THE
RESPONSIBILITY
OF THE
CHRISTIAN MUSICIAN

GLENN KAISER

Cornerstone Press Chicago
Chicago, Illinois

Published by Cornerstone Press Chicago, the publishing arm of Jesus People USA Covenant Church. Jesus People USA is a community of Christians serving the poor, the homeless, and the elderly in the Uptown neighborhood of Chicago. On a national and international level, Jesus People is known for Cornerstone magazine, the bands on the Grrr recordS label (REZ, Cauzin' efekt, CRASHDOG, and the Crossing), and Cornerstone Festival. If you would like more information about Jesus People USA and its outreaches, write JPUSA care of Cornerstone Press Chicago, 939 W. Wilson Ave., Chicago, IL 60640.

Scripture taken from the HOLY BIBLE, NEW INTERNATIONAL VERSION. Copyright © 1973, 1978, 1984 International Bible Society. Used by permission of Zondervan Bible Publishers.

ISBN 0-940895-21-8
Printed in the United States of America.
97   96   95   94   4   3   2   1

Cover design by Janet Cameron and Pat Peterson.

Library of Congress Cataloging-in-Publication Data

Kaiser, Glenn
  The responsibility of the Christian musician / Glenn Kaiser.
    p.   cm.
  ISBN 0-940895-21-8
  1. Church musicians--Conduct of life.   2. Church musicians-
-Religious life.   I. Title.
MT88.K29   1994
248.8'9--dc20   94-24995
                                                              CIP
                                                              MN

to Jesus
my Strength and Song

to Wendi
my Dearest Friend

to Rebecca, Heidi, and Amy
my Greatest Gifts

Contents

Preface

A vast percentage of God's Word deals with attitudes and relationships. Our personal relationship (or lack of one) with God is first and of greatest importance. Out from that relationship and into all others we bring our talents, sharing together in this thing called "life."

What a difference between heaven and hell! We as Christians are children of heaven. Our values, motives, and goals must mature into heaven's values, motives, and goals. This takes all the time God gives us! But praise Him—He is the author and finisher, the pioneer and perfecter of our faith (Heb. 12:2). This is the case for all believers.

Though his calling is the same, the Christian musician is at times a "lame duck" in the body of Christ. He or she is in a very strained environment both socially and spiritually. Throughout history, the Church has debated strongly over the artist and his gifts. Music and its use/abuse has been, and will always be, a controversial subject among Christians.

On the one hand, I believe part of what we are dealing with is rebellious young Christians who lack respect for the traditional church structures. They have stumbled over the cultural "norms" of the older generation. Yet, on the other hand, the traditional church in some quarters completely "unchristianizes" young musicians due to their style of music. This is a compound fracture. It is prejudice versus prejudice.

Many believers have disobeyed Scripture by refusing to fellowship with other Christians because of a non-scriptural disagreement over musical tastes. What can one say or do to end this unbiblical separation of brothers?

"For we know in part. . . . But the greatest of these is love" (1 Cor. 13:9, 13). If these scriptures are true, I individually, as well as we corporately, only "know in part." Why do we insist we are so completely right? Pride? Insecurity? Ignorance? Foolishness? My heart is for those most like myself. We all seem to share these afflictions. Yet to truly love, pray for, even fellowship in the Lord with those with whom we disagree is a testimony neither the world nor Satan can silence, regardless of the tune. Thank God musical taste is not a biblical ground for either fellowship or disfellowship! Sadly, some on either side of any given musical argument seem to think it is.

Where in the Word of God can this position be validated?

The truth is that both sides have much in common and much to learn from one another!

I praise God for those teachers, pastors, youth pastors, and music directors in the body of Christ who have carried the flame of truth, the Word of God, to young musicians—how absolutely necessary, for there is clearly great power and influence in music. Praise, testimony, and prophetic songs alike wield the sword of the Spirit with great effect. Yet how rarely do I hear this voice crying for solid biblical concepts to be made available to the younger or newer Christian musicians. It is one thing to know how to write, arrange, produce, and perform music. It is quite another thing to know how to live biblically in the process. Musicians, your lives and gifts will affect so many to such a deep extent! "From everyone who has been given much, much will be demanded" (Luke 12:48).

The Bible plainly teaches the responsibility of the Christian. Musicians are *not* exempt.

Because of the very communicativeness of our art form and the position it holds in society today, Christian musicians must be even more responsible with their lives and works of art. We musicians have tremendous potential as yielded vessels of the Holy Spirit . . . or as agents of nonsense . . . and even destruction. Idolatry takes many forms. Some of us bow to our culture as if it were Christ!

Do you worship the creation and created things (i.e., music) rather than the Creator? It is as valid a question for the older Christian as it is for the younger. Does God get an hour per week out of you (if that!), and your music rehearsal/listening about thirty or forty hours weekly? Be honest.

Many musicians are, frankly, one-dimensional. They constantly listen to, perform, talk about, read about, watch (on the tube), and dream *music* and almost nothing but music. Most of their friends are either musicians or groupies of some sort. Sounds like a balanced, well-rounded life doesn't it? What do you talk about most? Does most of your extra money go to missions and church needs or music and entertainment? What can you bring into an encounter with other Christians for you all to enjoy, grow from, and fellowship around? If music is your sole answer, you have some repenting . . . and growing up to do. It's all right. So do all of us. As born-again believers, we are all brothers and sisters. One of the marks of Christian maturity and love is the ability to "put away childish things." Do we musicians "play" while others truly "work"? Among Christians, especially, this must change. Proceed with caution. My prayer is that John 15:8 will become a reality in your life and music!

GLENN KAISER

Chapter One

RESPONSIBILITY TO YOUR FATHER, GOD

You were bought at a price; do not become slaves of men. Brothers, each man, as responsible to God, should remain in the situation God called him to (1 Cor. 7:23, 24).

It can be a very difficult thing to serve God in His confirmed calling, or it can be a fairly simple and satisfying, even easy thing. In reality it is both. What is it for you? The first and most important commandment according to Jesus Christ is: "Hear, O Israel, the Lord our God, the Lord is one. Love the Lord your God with all your heart and with all your soul and with all your mind and with all your strength" (Mark 12:29, 30). God says He is the one true (one and only) God and must be loved totally and completely. He says He is a jealous God and that we are to "have no other gods before" Him (Exod. 20:3)! So our first responsibility is not to others—be they born-again Christians or heathen sinners—not to ourselves, not to our work or calling! Our first and foremost responsibility is and always must be to God Himself.

It is the Word of God that makes us responsible. It can be safely said that our Christian life begins in the heart and mind of God. He created us. He loved us

2

deeply, but because of our sin we were separated from Him. He sacrificed His only Son on the cross that the penalty for our sin could be paid in full, thus opening the way for us to have a genuine eternal relationship with Him. But where does our responsibility start? "Hear, O Israel . . ." We have got to learn how to listen.

This word *responsible* has deep meaning and many implications. Webster's defines it as "liable to be called on to answer; able to answer for one's conduct and obligations: trustworthy; able to choose for oneself between right and wrong; marked by or involving responsibility or accountability." *Response* is the root word of this adjective. To reply, react, and respond to those with whom we enter a relationship is extremely important. In fact, we cannot have a relationship with someone if we don't in some way respond. If the Lord Jesus was anything at all, He was certainly responsible to do what He knew to be the will of the Father: "to do the will of Him who sent me" (John 6:38). When He was asked what the most important commandment was, He spoke about loving the Father supremely. This action of loving God is the stuff of life! The particular reply, reaction, and response we offer to the Lord when we believe He has spoken to us is the essence of our relationship with Him.

How do we hear His voice? He speaks personally to us through His Word (the Bible), as we pray, through our pastors/spiritual leaders (other Christians), via circumstances, and also through supernatural "signs and wonders." Once we are relatively sure of His direction we must act accordingly. It is at this point in the relationship that we either do or not do His will. If we make the right choices, our witness both to the world and to other Christians can foster a deeper understanding of God's love. Charles Colson's excellent book *Loving God* will provide even deeper insight into this phenomenon if you'd care to read further. My point is simple: many believers don't realize that they can never love in the fullest human sense unless they first allow Jesus to touch their hearts, minds, and souls with His heart, mind, and soul. It takes time. It can be frightening, even painful. But it is this time spent with God that makes the very spirit of the Christian sing! And the nature of the Christian becomes more like the One with whom he or she has spent his or her time. This fellowship eventually affects every aspect of life, including music if you are a musician.

We were indeed "bought at a price" (1 Cor. 6:20; 7:23). That price was the shed blood of a Lamb without spot, the blood of Jesus the Son of God—God the Son. The very blood of God was spilled that we might come home to Him in a loving Father to child relationship. To love, to serve, and to be faithful is our new responsibility, speaking honestly to Him each day in every situation, searching His book for guidance in all things pertaining to this life and eternity to come, listening to Him, obeying Him. This two-way relationship must be the foundation upon which the genuine Christian musician builds everything.

Becoming a slave to the whims of anyone else (including one's self) is not God's idea of being responsible to Him. This loyalty to God doesn't mean we offhandedly reject what others tell us. Yet at times our loyalty to God's call will divide us from others. This can be most painful, but it is a pain Jesus also felt in His obedience to God.

Being obedient to God is a part of the process of loving Him, receiving from Him the fuller sense of the acceptance He offers. This deeper experiencing of His constant love for you, personally, will free you to use His acceptance of you to help you accept and love others.

As your need for acceptance is filled and satisfied, you have the liberty not only to love Him, but also His children—be they lost or found. There is a liberty to love others when you are secure in His love and calling in your own life. You are more able to minister support and biblical "brotherly affection" towards people who don't like you or what you are doing musically.

Because He loves them, so do I. Because I am experiencing His love for me, I don't have to worry about me! I can work for others to help them more fully come into His love for them. We love Him "because He first loved us" (1 John 4:19). When we are about the action and interaction of discovering His love and actually communicating it back to Him...what peace and joy! What worship and adoration results! This is a romance deeper than any other and from which all other romance must spring. Out of these moments will come music that is God-inspired and God-glorifying! It may be a shout or a whisper, but it will speak to the heart of man because it is born out of a relationship with the very Creator of the creation, the Creator of creativity!

There are volumes of excellent books available on our multidimensional relationship with God. Let's take a moment to list a few specific modes of communication God has given us to help us grow in relationship with Him:

• Listening. This would include reading the Bible, good devotional or biblically sound teaching books, etc. Also, it includes realizing when it is Him speaking to us through other people, creation, circumstance, and miracles.

• Speaking. What is truly amazing is that the Creator of the universe listens to us! We speak to Him in prayer, of course. Yet we also speak to Him by our deepest thoughts and actions.

• Presence. The meaning of the word *presence* is attendance, close proximity. Sometimes there is such a sense of His presence it is incredible. Some even remark that they physically sense Him "with" them. Certainly this is one dimension of the Holy Spirit's work in the life of the believer, and it is a part of the whole of our relationship with the Father.

What is not mentioned enough is that this multi-dimensional relationship with God takes time! Many Christians seem to think these truths are so biblically evident that the new Christian just "gets it." Of course, Jesus loves and accepts you. This is the basis of your faith in Him for salvation. But living in the everyday real world, this basic faith and security in His care and protection will be tested.

Praise be to the God and Father of our Lord Jesus Christ! In His great mercy He has given us new birth into a living hope through the resurrection of Jesus Christ from the dead, and into an inheritance that can never perish, spoil or fade—kept in heaven for you, who through faith are shielded by God's power until the coming of the salvation that is ready to be revealed in the last time. In this you greatly rejoice, though now for a little while you may have had to suffer grief in all kinds of trials. These have come so that your faith—of greater worth than gold, which perishes even though refined by fire—may be proved genuine and may result in praise, glory and honor when Jesus Christ is revealed. Though you have not seen Him, you love Him; and even though you do not see Him now, you believe in Him and are filled with an inexpressible and glorious joy, for you are receiving the goal of your faith, the salvation of your souls (1 Pet. 1:3–9; *see also* 1 Pet. 4:12).

And it will grow. But growth takes time. Very few things (if any) are instant in the Christian life. So you must learn to work at your spiritual life in order to deepen your trust and experience of God's faithfulness. If you will, a wonderful thing will begin to happen. You will see your relationship with God grow into real, God-honoring, soul-satisfying worship.

Worship is something we can never do enough of, something we are indeed always doing in a sense, and something through which we grow ourselves and through which we grow in God. I have long stated that one of the problems of the contemporary Christian music crowd (musicians and audience alike) is that we know how to enjoy our music . . . but do we know how to worship? Of course many Christians think they worship when in fact they only go through the motions. If step one is to worship, then step two is to do it genuinely and from the heart. And some say that in a typical Christian concert they are worshiping Jesus right there! Sometimes yes, sometimes no. Because it has to do with a heart attitude more than anything else, it takes serious discernment to know whether someone is truly praising God or simply reacting emotionally to a given stimulus. Naturally (and

I do mean in the sense of "natural man"), there are those who "discern" with a very human bias.

But there is something deeper yet. It is not only my privilege but also my duty (duty: giving God His due) to worship Him. It is also one of my greatest joys. In song, in silence, with or without a sense of His presence, I worship Him. He is worthy! Amen, worthy, worthy, and worthy of the deepest, highest praise, thanksgiving, and worship. When we see His face on that Day we will most certainly reach a level of worship which at the present time we have only a hint. I love Jesus! I adore Him! He is the most wonderful person who is! And in those times of worship, not only do I try to discover new as well as old ways of telling Him all of this, but also He ministers to me in a thousand ways that cause me to better understand *why* I love Him so—and why I must love Him more and better still.

Possibly the best songs are sung in our hearts to Him. They are for no one else, nor can they be. Neither are they in any way for us. They are pure, chaste, holy offerings of love. Simple, genuine gifts to His majesty. Notes, rhythms, and words that express adoration toward the Most Adorable, Most High, Most Powerful, Most Holy King of kings, and Lord of lords. Begin here. Return here, to this attitude. From this relationship all others will be touched.

So we have cause to rejoice in our calling (1 Cor. 7:23,

24). If that happens to be music, so be it. There is no shame in it. Only when we separate ourselves from the God who does the calling do we, and those around us affected by that calling, suffer. When our lives are at peace within God and His will, we can then reach out through our callings to draw others to Him. Some will hear and respond, some will not. But our first love must be toward and for our Lord. As we explore all of the depths and mysteries of our communion with Him, others will be touched, because this interaction in our lives will naturally seep into our music. If it doesn't, our relationship and therefore our responsibility to God must be questioned. Times like that are not for making music. They are silent. When things are as they should be with our Lord again—we sing!

Chapter Two

Responsibility to Your Family

Growing Up at Home

Children, obey your parents in the Lord, for this is right. "Honor your father and mother"—which is the first command-ment with a promise—"that it may go well with you and that you may enjoy long life on the earth."

Fathers, do not exasperate your children; instead, bring them up in the training and instruction of the Lord (Eph. 6:1–4).

Certainly, one of the hardest things we each have to go through in our lives is to grow up in the kind of society that we now live in! No doubt, it can be very frustrat-ing to find that one of the things you get most pleasure out of—your music—is one of the most debated topics in your home.

All of us have to face the fact that one day we'll grow up, probably get married, have children of our own, and repeat the whole crazy process, except we'll give our chil-dren more understanding and freedom than our parents gave us, right? Nope! Don't believe it for a minute!

All of us agree sometimes and disagree other times about a lot of things. And on occasion we think our par-ents are as dumb as they seem to think we are. Many of them don't know Guns n' Roses from Michael Card. (No offense, Michael, I like you a whole lot more.) And they think that our desire to play our kind of music our way is sinful in general, rebellious in particular. Besides that, they just don't like it and either can't figure out why we do or act as if they do know the reasons we like it—and good Christians don't like things for those reasons. Or something like that.

Well, let me tell you about how it was growing up at my house. After we dig through some of my story we will think about yours and see how we differ and how we are alike. And then we'll think more about the hassles we go through growing up as musicians at home. My family was pretty typical in some ways: midwestern, middle class, and living at first in a small town, then moving to a pretty average suburb of a larger city. We children went to public schools and were average students who could have done better but didn't study because we didn't care much about it. We spent a lot of time with our friends and had a dog—you get the picture. So my parents divorced, my sister got married, and my brother joined the army and married later on. I was the youngest of the three children.

My mom had been a gifted singer at one time, before cigarettes and other things helped end that. As a high school girl she had won singing contests in Milwaukee and played piano and accordion quite well. My dad had played sax in dance bands and they both liked music, although I don't remember a great deal of it being played in our house when I was growing up. My brother and sister listened to pop music when I was quite young. But my teenage years were spent without their influence because they were both gone from home by then. My mom listened to Judy Garland, Sinatra, Mantovani, stuff like that. Frankly, I thought it was okay. I liked so many different kinds of music and styles within each genre that I amazed myself! And to this day, the only style I rather dislike is jazz . . . and I even like certain forms of that.

I was always basically fat, outgoing, and very lost. I had lots of friends and spent tons of time listening to the radio and watching TV, but from here on out the facts get a bit weirder. You see, when you're insecure and you feel as if you have only one good thing going for you, you push it for all it's worth. I could sing. I could play a lot of instruments, at least fairly well. And as soon as I tried, I found I could write music and lyrics, get into bands, start my own bands, and finally be somebody cool.

To be cool is important when in your heart you really wonder why you're alive at all. Nobody in my family had ever been a genuine, practicing Christian. I had a lot of deep hurts and doubts about whether I was "worth the powder to blow myself up." And, with the one exception of my music, I didn't think I was. Then, before my last year in high school, I lost sixty pounds during a summer of not eating and doing a lot of drugs. I was a mess, destroying myself. And when I went back to school the next fall . . . fall I did!

The best thing that could have happened to me just about killed me. The first day back to school nobody knew I was me! All the weight was gone, and suddenly the one group of people with whom I had never had the kind of relationship I'd always wanted—well, girls—started to seem to like me, and not just like friends, you know? Sure I liked it, but you have to understand that I didn't even realize when somebody was flirting with me. I mean, it had never happened to me before!

When everyone in your family has cheated and been cheated on and you grow up without any real understanding of God's words and ways, you get hurt easy, you hurt others, and you *run* from commitments. I didn't really trust girls. I didn't trust anyone. And I learned that I couldn't trust myself either.

Music was a constant friend. I wanted rock stars to love me. I thought they kind of did. They talked about the same things I thought and talked about all the time. They understood a lot about life . . . or so I thought. And music didn't force itself on me. It did what I made it do. If I did or didn't want to listen to something, I just turned the dial or hit the switch or walked into or out of the concert. Simple.

Nothing else in my life or in any of the lives around me made so much sense as my music. Nothing else gave me so much happiness or sense of purpose until I asked Jesus Christ to come into my heart and become the absolute Lord of my life. But before that day, music was the one thing in my empty life that seemed to continually help fill the void inside.

That's my history. I promised I would talk about your family next and try to deal with some of the hassles we all go through as musicians at home.

From following Jesus, I learned a few good lessons early: Don't fight about music. If you and your family have differences perhaps talking with a youth pastor you both trust might help, but I'm serious—if you and your family can't talk your differences over "in the Spirit," forget it! You're going to be sinning (either or all of you) if you simply argue about musical tastes over and over again. Pray. Obey your parents. Don't lose Jesus for the sake of music! Don't make music your idol. Idolatry is listed in several places in the Bible as a way to end up in hell, so be serious about prayer and obedience to your parents. Be careful to spend as much time on Jesus and others as you do on music . . . or you are going to be out of balance just like some of the people you'd like to argue with! Music is a lousy substitute for Bible study, prayer, genuine spiritual Christian discussion, and witnessing to people about the Lord Jesus. Face it. It's true. Do you want it to "go well with you"? Reread the verses at the beginning of this chapter. Really work at being as honest about your true motives as you can. When you are legally "of age" and at the point that you are out of your parents' house, you'll be free to express yourself musically under God and biblically as you see fit. It seems like forever, but that time will come soon enough. Consider God's wisdom in these words:

> I say to myself, "The Lord is my portion; therefore I will wait for Him." The Lord is good to those whose hope is in Him, to the one who seeks Him; it is good to wait quietly for the salvation of the Lord. It is good for a man to bear the yoke while he is young (Lam. 3:24–27).

That yoke is an easy yoke according to Jesus: "Take my yoke upon you and learn from me, for I am gentle and humble in heart, and you will find rest for your souls. For my yoke is easy and my burden is light." (Matt. 11:29, 30). But it doesn't seem like it sometimes. When we can grow into the gentleness and humility of Jesus, we can rest in Him whether our parents let us "go for it" musically or not. Read Hebrews 12:5–14.

And you have forgotten that word of encouragement that addresses you as sons:

> "My son, do not make light of the Lord's discipline, and do not lose heart when He rebukes you, because the Lord disciplines those He loves, and He punishes everyone He accepts as a son."

Endure hardship as discipline; God is treating you

as sons. For what son is not disciplined by his father? If you are not disciplined (and everyone undergoes discipline), then you are illegitimate children and not true sons. Moreover, we have all had human fathers who disciplined us and we respected them for it. How much more should we submit to the Father of our spirits and live! Our fathers disciplined us for a little while as they thought best; but God disciplines us for our good, that we may share in His holiness. No discipline seems pleasant at the time, but painful. Later on, however, it produces a harvest of righteousness and peace for those who have been trained by it.

Therefore, strengthen your feeble arms and weak knees. "Make level paths for your feet," so that the lame may not be disabled, but rather healed.

Make every effort to live in peace with all men and to be holy; without holiness no one will see the Lord.

Discipline, holiness, and right living are essentials, not options, for Christians. Think of Jesus on the cross, and then consider surrendering where your parents ask you to in this part of your musical life. Which is worse? We don't know what suffering really means! But love, and prayer, and living by the Word of our Father in heaven will help us to be the examples that our families need to encourage them to grow in the Lord too. "Don't let anyone look down on you because you are young, but set an example for the believers in speech, in life, in love, in faith and in purity" (1 Tim. 4:12).

Parents can exasperate their children. God tells them not to do it, but they sin in this way sometimes. They don't train and instruct their children in the Lord to the extent they should. If these mistakes are made in the preachers' families, how much more in homes where Mom and/or Dad isn't even a Bible-believing Christian?

My wife and I have four of the best children on the planet. We love them with all of our hearts. We pray for them constantly and struggle to help them make biblical choices. Sometimes we both exasperate each other. But "love covers over all wrongs" (Prov. 10:12). We have learned to ask forgiveness when either of us has wronged the other. If you "make love your aim," you will find that music will take its proper place. You may even learn to like styles you never cared about before.

And remember, there will soon come a day when you will do just as your parents did when they came of age. You will be free to listen to and, as a musician, perform whatever you wish. Study the Scriptures for a good understanding of what God says about music. Learn to worship. Learn to listen. There is a future time for expression to the fullest. By then, you hopefully will have learned that your parents will not be judged by God for their influence on your musical direction. When you are on your own, you alone will have to face His judgment of your motives.

From that time on, there will be no one else to blame.

Thank God for parents who understand, who know the Word and refuse to let their personal desires dictate your musical pursuits. But others of you must also thank God for parents who are at least trying to teach you their values because, to the best of their knowledge, their values are right. Right or not, caring parents are better than those who could care less about how you grow, if you grow, or where you end up! Think it through. Many people wish they had parents as good as yours.

Many more wish they had a Father in heaven like yours, even though they may not realize they feel that way. Music is only one way of telling them about Him. There are other ways—in fact, much better ways. Interestingly enough, Jesus is not mentioned as being much of a musician or even a singer. But I love Him exactly as the Book reveals Him whether or not He uses me in music. Jesus Christ *is* my life; music-making is simply one of the things I do to obey Him. It is one act of worship among several. But while growing up at home, it must be balanced with obeying your parents because God commands both! Up to this point, what I have been saying can be applied equally to either male or female performers. From now on my male viewpoint will restrict my applications more. For instance, I will not be able to write about the special problems that a married woman performer might have, although much of what I have to say will apply.

Married

I would like you to be free from concern. An unmarried man is concerned about the Lord's affairs—how he can please the Lord. But a married man is concerned about the affairs of this world—how he can please his wife—and his interests are divided. An unmarried woman or virgin is concerned about the Lord's affairs: Her aim is to be devoted to the Lord in both body and spirit. But a married woman is concerned about the affairs of this world—how she can please her husband. I am saying this for your own good, not to restrict you, but that you may live in a right way in undivided devotion to the Lord (1 Cor. 7:32–35).

Let me get right to the point: it ain't easy! Some people dream about marrying a Christian musician and all of the attached "glories" that are supposedly a part of our lifestyle. Others wonder why they ever married a musician in the first place. Serving God in a music ministry is at times a most costly thing. Before you marry, be as certain as possible that your proposed mate is willing to share the expense.

Too many people have stars in their eyes and, quite frankly, rocks in their head. It is clear from the history of Gospel music, the shorter history of contemporary Christian music, and from the record of the traveling evangelist and pulpit pastor alike: those who do not share the same calling are sure to share a definite misery. The lonely hours, mothers left at home to raise the children, constant travel, and living out of a suitcase can really take their toll on a marriage.

Before we got married, I told Wendi about every possible twist I could anticipate in the future of our music ministry. I tried to paint as honest a picture as I could of what marrying me would cost her, specifically, because of the call of God on my life. I wanted to give her the option to follow the Lord if He had called her to another way. The last thing I wanted was for her to be hurt by God's call to this narrower road. I shared what I believed was the future plan of God for REZ—the vision. And after all of this, she said yes.

Something many people are still learning is that marriage is as much a matter of obedience and making a right choice as it is a matter of "love." They are so moved by their emotions or by a romantic notion of love—being in love with love itself—that they don't ask themselves or their proposed mates the hard questions about future costs. Discipleship costs. Marriage, like discipleship, costs. Yet both are very real blessings.

You must understand that, at the time, we had no idea that the Lord would "draft" her into the band. So her prospect of following me around the world to a lot of strange places where REZ would minister did not include going as an actual member of the group. She basically told me, "Where you go I will go, where you stay I will stay." It is a godly woman indeed who will live out that kind of unselfish commitment. Brothers in ministry—

marry a minister! Sisters in ministry—do the same!

One of the most practical blessings of traveling with a spouse who is a minister is that they can be called upon to talk to someone of the opposite sex if the individual either wants or needs to get into deeper conversation. If the topic at hand isn't proper for you to discuss with them or if you just get the sense that what they really want is attention and a chance to flirt, your wife is the one they should talk to. I have thanked the Lord many times for Wendi's place in REZ and in my marriage in this respect!

A fair amount of prayer, fasting, and confirmation from others took place before the band was formed. The same serious asking, seeking, and knocking for clear guidance took place before we were married. I have never been sorry or ashamed about that. When you are genuinely working at daily living a life based on obedience to God rather than personal desire, you find it much easier to trust Him to meet the various needs. You then live in greater peace and security.

Suffering and sacrifice are a part of life. Jesus is our supreme example of this. "Greater love has no one than this, that he lay down his life for his friends" (John 15:13). What are the ramifications of this verse when we consider a Christian musician who is married? Earlier, I mentioned a few of the practical struggles. Let's briefly consider a few more.

No wife likes to hear her husband lambasted by church leaders because of the method through which he believes God has led him to minister. No husband likes to leave a wife alone in a house or apartment for fear of any number of things that could happen while he is away. She is then the one to face the monthly (weekly?) bills and creditors. She is the one who wonders about his purity as he travels in a world of lonely, broken lives. He wonders if her position in a secular business is really the best place for her. There are so many scenarios in the real world that I probably don't need to discuss the car breaking down while he is away, the plumbing failures, etc., etc. It isn't easy for her to know that he gets security and approval from the audience while she gets four square walls and a few (if any) girlfriends who may not really understand the couple's calling enough to biblically encourage her through the dark times.

The other option is for a married couple to travel together. And in that situation all of the physical, spiritual, and emotional pressures of "road life" are shared. Depending on your situation, a different bed, town, church or crowd, promoter, and a large number of hurt lives and tough situations will have to be faced daily. Sound like your idea of a good time? Now you have to worry about spending quality time with her because if she's working in the group or with sound or concessions or whatever, she is as much "in demand" as you are.

Though traveling together, you are unable to *be* together much until late at night when you're both too worn-out to do much but pray yourselves to sleep!

And then there are rehearsals, interviews, and much more. It can be quite tiring after a while—not to mention downtimes when there are few concerts to do. For many, it is very difficult having to change their daily pattern, readjusting to being "normal" for a while. Ask anyone in music ministry if these things are not so. We are to be perfect examples at all times, yet there are moments we question whether or not we are even functioning marriage partners!

I have stated many times in the past that when God calls you to minister to others, you must understand that your life is truly no longer yours alone. Those in any type of public ministry are responsible not only to God and their church but also, in another sense, for those to whom God sends them. It is demanding at times. But if it is the will of God for you to serve in music or another public ministry, you must learn how to be an unselfish steward of your time. If married, you will both have to learn how to do this.

Now some foundations for those married or seriously considering it. If you have received a clear, confirmed calling to be involved in some aspect of music ministry, you had better do some serious praying and talking about it with your spouse or spouse-to-be. Depending upon how he or she responds, you will have to decide who you are serving first. I made it absolutely clear many years ago that I was not going to backslide out of what I was certain to be the will of God for my life—for anyone. I must say it again, and say it clearly: Few ministers bother to advise young would-be preachers or music ministers, etc., to either stay single or marry a person who is as called of God and committed to service as you are.

God hates divorce. There are biblical grounds for it, yet it is not in His heart for separation to take place between those He has united.

> Some Pharisees came to Him to test Him. They asked, "Is it lawful for a man to divorce his wife for any and every reason?"
>
> "Haven't you read," He replied, "that at the beginning the Creator 'made them male and female,' and said, 'For this reason a man will leave his father and mother and be united to his wife, and the two will become one flesh'? So they are no longer two, but one. Therefore what God has joined together, let man not separate."
>
> "Why then," they asked, "did Moses command that a man give his wife a certificate of divorce and send her away?"
>
> Jesus replied, "Moses permitted you to divorce your wives because your hearts were hard. But it was not this way from the beginning. I tell you that anyone who divorces his wife, except for marital unfaithful-

ness, and marries another woman commits adultery."

The disciples said to Him, "If this is the situation between a husband and wife, it is better not to marry."

Jesus replied, "Not everyone can accept this word, but only those to whom it has been given. For some are eunuchs because they were born that way; others were made that way by men; and others have renounced marriage because of the kingdom of heaven. The one who can accept this should accept it (Matt. 19:3–12).

One of the few just claims being leveled at music (and other) ministers today is that the divorce rate among them speaks to the obvious hypocrisy in one or both of their lives. How can we respond to this? With secure, single service in Christ. Or, as in my own situation, with a solid marriage based on biblical principles, submitted to a church where there is good marriage counseling available whenever needed.

There are only two other options, and neither are good. You either divorce or you follow God's will in ministry service. Do you really want to get into that kind of a situation? Do you want to go through or put another human being through that kind of hell on earth? God is more important than marriage. And marriage is more important than self.

The hard realities of Christian service have caused many to sour in their hearts. A "root of bitterness" has sprung up, and many have not only been defiled by it, but they have also done damage to the way unbelievers think about Jesus and His gospel. Take a hard look at Hebrews 12:12–17.

> Therefore, strengthen your feeble arms and weak knees. "Make level paths for your feet," so that the lame may not be disabled, but rather healed.
>
> Make every effort to live in peace with all men and to be holy; without holiness no one will see the Lord. See to it that no one misses the grace of God and that no bitter root grows up to cause trouble and defile many. See that no one is sexually immoral, or is godless like Esau, who for a single meal sold his inheritance rights as the oldest son. Afterward, as you know, when he wanted to inherit this blessing, he was rejected. He could bring about no change of mind, though he sought the blessing with tears.

We are to strengthen, make level paths, make every effort to live in peace and to be holy. We are to see to it that no one misses the grace of God. We are to watch out for that root of bitterness. *We* are to "see that no one is sexually immoral, or is godless like Esau," and it is our problem. These verses clearly accent our responsibility. God is forever responsible for what He does. And we will also face the consequences of our actions. With all of this in mind, I recommend the following:

(1) Establish daily (unless really impossible) prayer and

Bible study with your partner if you are seriously contemplating both marriage and Christian service.

(2) Establish an ongoing relationship (or at the very least, get in touch) with those who have strong marriages and are serving the Lord in Christian music ministry. Ask them honest questions. Get some experienced, biblically sound answers.

(3) Establish a commitment to a strong church where biblical counseling is available. I'll tell you a sad fact of life: in a young marriage (and sometimes even an older marriage that had a bad or weak foundation), couples just don't know how to attack the problem. They lash out at each other. The Book says we don't fight flesh and blood, but Satan will do his best (worst?) to tell us the opposite. For this I offer a solution: an accountable relationship with a godly party who is outside the marriage and who doesn't stand to gain or lose anything in the particular argument—someone who truly loves you both. They can help you argue biblically. They can help you find solutions. The other option here is the one that too many couples take: they hide in their little bunker of a "home" and just fight like cats and dogs . . . all alone. Sure, it's nobody's business but yours—unless you're part of a church that's going to move biblically on sin and confront it!

Are we our brother's keeper? What is hypocrisy? How do we "carry each other's burdens, and in this way ... fulfill the law of Christ" (Gal. 6:2) and not get involved with battling couples in our churches? If you can figure out a better way to love, express love, and bring biblical solutions to a hurting marriage be sure and write or phone me, because I'm a pastor who desperately wants to know how to biblically serve my congregation! Too many Christians have missed the truth that we don't have to be at the point of separation to need to talk over biblical principles of growth for our marriages. And by the way, both of you need the humility to face this fact. In other words, if one of you thinks it's time to talk things out with a pastor or older Christian, you both ought to do it!

(4) Read whatever books you can about these issues. There are many available. Most pastors and any Christian bookstore can help you find some. A few that we have found helpful are *The Christian Family* by Larry Christenson, anything by Dr. James Dobson and Dr. Ed Wheat. These will at least provide a starting point for further study.

If Satan wants to do anything, it is to destroy relationships. The first relationship he wants to erode is the one you share with God. Next on his hit list is your marriage. Sometimes, the best way to get at someone is not directly, but through their family. This is what every believer—therefore, Christian musician—is up against.

When my wife and I were first married, we experienced this continually. Our commitments to Jesus, to each other, and to His calling (evangelizing and discipling via music ministry) were constantly tested. Those early times of prayer, Bible study, and discussion and our church's input into our lives via teaching, counseling, and tapes, etc., really saw us through the "rapids." We were very young, quite stubborn, and fairly proud—and therefore, argumentative! Still, we were able to remain faithful to each important relationship (which, if you haven't guessed yet, is what this book is really all about) because of all of the foundational "cement." We have always had people in our church family (Jesus People USA) who have prayed for, encouraged, and, yes, corrected us when we have been in danger of getting off the path. What's more, those who have given us the most open rebuke have also proven to be our best and closest friends. Consider the two following bits of wisdom from Proverbs 27:5, 6: "Better is open rebuke than hidden love. Wounds from a friend can be trusted." There are no great secrets to acquiring marital stability for musicians. It comes by thought and hard work. It takes time. And it happens as you both establish and maintain biblical patterns of living and biblical relationships. This, of course, is easier said than done. But it is neither impossible nor beyond the scope of any of us. For in some ways the couple involved in music ministry is no different than any other Christian couple. God's grace is sufficient! "But he said to me, 'My grace is sufficient for you, for my power is made perfect in weakness.' Therefore I will boast all the more gladly about my weaknesses, so that Christ's power may rest on me" (2 Cor. 12:9).

Raising Children

Fathers, do not exasperate your children; instead bring them up in the training and instruction of the Lord (Eph. 6:4).

He will turn the hearts of the fathers to their children, and the hearts of the children to their fathers; or else I will come and strike the land with a curse (Mal. 4:6).

In the Book of Psalms are three verses that I know and truly love: "Sons are a heritage from the Lord, children a reward from him. Like arrows in the hands of a warrior are sons born in one's youth. Blessed is the man whose quiver is full of them. They will not be put to shame when they contend with their enemies in the gate" (Ps. 127:3–5).

If the Lord brings children into your marriage, you'll be amazed at the blessings that will accompany them! Children really are special to a family. But because of them, you will also be stretched literally to the breaking point. Certainly, any relationship worth having is going to cost something. And I must tell you that for the Christian musician, children will radically change your perspective and your ministry.

Let's begin with Psalm 127.

Children are serious gifts! When God brought my children into my life, I entered into a new experience of learning that hasn't stopped yet—and it's been many years since our first child arrived on the scene.

Some people grow up around children, but I didn't. Not only was I the youngest in my family, I can't say I ever remember my older sister baby-sitting or anything like that. So there were just never any little children in my life.

As I got older and hung out at friends' houses, I got acquainted with some of their younger brothers or sisters, but only in a very surface way. So you see, in terms of practical experience, I just wasn't prepared for the responsibility of having children. But God decided He could educate me! Four children and many years later, I believe He knew what He was doing and how He would get it done.

Each one of my children turned out to be a very real gift to Wendi and I. They share similarities and, yet, each of them is truly an individual with his or her own unique personality. But let me tell you, my wife and the other pastors in our church really helped me learn to relate to them. I don't know what would have happened without their encouragement and support.

Let me explain.

I was very much involved in both ministry and hobbies as our children came along. And I was just young, immature, and selfish enough to not want to spend time kid-watching when I could be doing something that I considered more fulfilling. Not being around children all my life, I didn't exactly know *how* to interact with them. I didn't know what to *do* with them! But God began to show me, through personal confrontation and also via my wife and pastors, how important it was for me to grow up and face the responsibilities of fatherhood.

Scriptures like those that opened this chapter just leaped off of the pages of my Bible during my personal devotions. I began to think about some of the traits of my own parents—good and bad—that I obviously and unknowingly shared. Again and again the Lord confronted me with the depths of my own selfish nature. Passages of Scripture (e.g., the twelfth chapter of Hebrews) had fresh meaning as I read them from a parent's perspective. Ultimately, God caused me to repent and finally come into new spiritual growth in a part of my life that He had scarcely touched before. Without children, it wouldn't have happened.

We normally advise people who marry to wait a few years before having their first child in order to build their marriage partnership on the Word and get established in a strong Bible-teaching church. Once a solid marriage foundation is built with prayer and scriptural guidance, they can begin raising a family.

Dr. James Dobson is one of a host of good counselors who offer excellent teaching on the family. There is no shortage of good Christian books on the subject. Read them. And at times, weep. Of course you'll be laughing a lot too! You'll be surprised how much you'll have in common with other married couples when you get together and in the course of fellowship, begin to share experiences God gave you with your children. Again, you can learn a lot just by talking with others who have had more experience with family life than you have.

Let's think about archery for a moment! Psalm 127 says children are "like arrows in the hands of a warrior." I have been involved in archery for several years. I learned a great little quote some years back: "He who never shoots, never misses." In other words, you're going to make mistakes no matter how hard you try. You *will* "exasperate them" sometimes. You *won't* have read the Word with them or given them godly instruction or set the most biblically sound example for them to follow all the time. That's a fact.

I'm not the best bow-shot on the block either. But God brought each of my children into this world and into my life, and I may only have a short time to influence them with biblical love, discipline, and instruction. So

I'm going for it while I can!

Practically speaking, we got in the habit of bringing our children out on the road with us as much as possible when they were younger. Now we plan our traveling schedule with regard to how much we'll be separated from our families. When it doesn't totally blow up their school studies, we take turns bringing them on tour. And when we're home, quality time spent with them is something we work at.

Again, I'm not the most natural "kid person" in the world, but I highly recommend good children's books. It's surprising how interesting *Timothy the Turtle* can be! Somewhere along the way I missed some of my childhood—so I'm making up for it now.

We take turns settling them at bedtime, reading to them, singing worship songs together, and praying together. We go to the park, play in the yard, or take them to the library or out for ice cream. Because everyone in REZ lives in community, we also have had an incredible amount of help from others who have baby-sat or worked as "nannies" when we couldn't take them along with us.

My wife and I talk about the "tag team" concept often. That's when the "little darlings" are driving you nuts, and it's just about time to do some serious praying! We try to pitch in for each other. For instance, if Wendi is up counseling late at night, I let her sleep in. I get up and have breakfast with the children, do our morning Scripture reading, and try to keep them from waking her up. We communicate about what to do so the children won't wear us out. I'm convinced that one of the reasons God provided two parents rather than one is that one alone just about "loses the victory" without the other's help!

It is real work supervising their playtime, helping with homework, establishing careful TV or video watching rules, and having serious talks about things that matter. But as we've often teased one another after a long day, "You knew the job was dangerous when you took it!" And we did. But we didn't know *how* dangerous! With abortion, child abuse and molestation, churches that at times treat children like second-class citizens, and with plain neglect, a message is being sent to today's children: growing up in a Christian home might not be much different than growing up in an unbelieving household. Or it might even be worse.

Malachi prophesied a mouthful, and we Christian parents had better take heed. As if this fallen world didn't have enough curses on it already, God said that unless fathers and their children allowed their hearts to be turned toward each other, one more curse would result. "He will turn the hearts of the fathers to their children, and the hearts of the children to their fathers; or else I will come and strike the land with a curse" (Mal. 4:6). His heart breaks for the Father/Son relationship to be re-created as much as is humanly possible in our families here on earth. But many musicians are too selfish, too ignorant, and too proud to do much about it. This must be addressed.

How often the adage haunts us about the people who win the world but lose their family in the process. It takes careful planning to establish and maintain balance.

Christian musicians who are also parents have a serious ministry "cut out for them." At times, it's a hard task trying to balance our writing, rehearsal, touring, recording, and family life. But I'll tell you what: what your children think of you is a thousand times more important than what someone else's children think of you and your Christianity!

If you have to travel without them, do your best to try to help them understand the practical reasons. Furthermore, be sure to have a serious talk with your children explaining *why* you minister and do what you do. Of course, if they are able to be with you, they can see it.

One of our children was taught about abortion in her Christian school. She came home talking about it, and when we realized that she had somehow missed the fact that it happens right here in America, we discussed it with her. She was really distressed. The next thing she said was that someone needed to do something to try and stop it. My wife explained that the abortion issue was one of the reasons we minister and travel so much. When people begin to follow Jesus and live by His Word, abortion, as well as other issues, find their solutions in Him. We adults understand this. Our children need to understand it, too.

Every family with parents involved in any type of ministry shares similar struggles. It takes much prayer, counsel, and a whole lot of grace. But I truly have been enriched through my relationship to my children.

Learning what it means to love them has taught me so much! It has brought into my life a deeper faith, a greater understanding of my dependence on God, and a clearer sense of the Father's heart towards me, my children, and yours. All of what God has done in my heart and life because of my children eventually filters into and through my music ministry as well.

If you are willing to die to self and follow Jesus as Lord and if you're willing to have your heart broken as well as filled, you can have both a vital music ministry and a strong family with children included! It's anything but dull!

And I highly recommend it.

Chapter Three

Responsibility to the Family of God

Local Church

Let us not give up meeting together, as some are in the habit of doing, but let us encourage one another—and all the more as you see the Day approaching (Heb. 10:25).

Unfortunately, the local church fellowship is often one of the last places the average musician can go to for a biblical sense of support regarding his or her vocation. Sad statement, isn't it? But too true. Most Christians have little knowledge of what Scripture has to say about music, musicianship, or musicians. Some of the most out-spoken preachers seem to be the most ignorant in these areas of biblical knowledge. The typical pastor has had little training (if any) on the biblical usage of music. I might add that many look at Christians who are serious about musical pursuits as sort of odd. Some don't consider a musical career a "real job." Others are simply functionalist: if it doesn't fit into the rather strict traditional format and the liturgy of the given church—forget it!

To say that many of us slice our lives into "sacred" and "secular" parts is an understatement. But if it is true that church-life and everyday life are to remain two separate and distinct parts of my Christian life, how can I possibly fulfill the scriptural mandate to "do it all for the glory of God" (1 Cor. 10:31)? The Church's doctrine of commitment needs far more biblical study and discussion than most Christians give it, and I am not as convinced as some that there are easy answers readily available. If it were all so clear, the Church wouldn't debate and disagree as much as it does. "How do I live my faith consistently in the everyday world?" is one of the continuing questions of the Church. Our witness and the potency/sterility of it may well rest upon our individual answers to these very questions. These are a few of the problems and issues associated with a Christian musician truly committing himself to a traditional church. But there is another side to this dilemma.

It takes no genius to realize that great numbers of Christian musicians simply aren't committed to a strong Bible-teaching church, or any church in their locality. This is clearly a violation of God's Word. Furthermore, very few within the musical groups are called or gifted in pastoring; therefore, a close relationship with the established leadership of a good church is one of the most important sources of sound teaching, checks and balances, encouragement, support, and safety. The Bible plainly teaches that all Christians are a part of the church and that pastoral care and oversight in an assembly of believers is a foundational part of our experience. In other words, if you have no pastor and home church you are either ignorant of what the Book says about this, rebellious against it, both of these, or not a Christian in the first place.

A brief Bible study will present the principles from which true Christians form habits: meeting together, submission to church authority, and the necessity for sound biblical teaching, instruction, and advice. Having honestly dealt with these truths, we must discuss some of the ramifications.

Let's say I decide to search out a Bible-based church in my area. For a number of reasons, I will never find the perfect church! Nor am I ever going to be considered the most "model" churchgoer/disciple of Christ that they have ever seen. This congregation doesn't seem to relate to me in general, because of my (their?) cultural tastes in dress and especially music. Must I change or must they? Or should I continue searching for the fellowship that most suits me for the rest of my life? The only real options are to plug into that church or not attend church. (A never-ending quest for a church that fits is a way of not attending church.) This last "option" is one many musicians choose all too often. The strongest arguments I have against that kind of choice are the following Scriptures:

> For where two or three come together in my name, there am I with them (Matt. 18:20).
>
> When the day of Pentecost came, they were all

together in one place (Acts 2:1).

> Submit to one another out of reverence for Christ (Eph. 5:21; *see also* Heb. 10:25; Mark 1:21; Luke 4:16; Acts 1:4, 14; 4:31; 1 Cor. 11:33; Heb. 13:7, 17; 1 Pet. 5:5; Prov. 11:14; 12:15; 13:10; 15:22; 20:18).

Some of you have considered throwing this book out the window, I'm sure. You are thinking about the exceptions to what I have just stated. No doubt, Christians in certain prisons, somebody shipwrecked on a tropical island, or someone living in a Moslem or other country where Christianity is outlawed come to mind. But when an individual in the Western nations reaches a given age, he or she is free to commute or to prayerfully relocate to another town or even state, find employment, and then join a fellowship where biblical Christian commitment is possible. In any event, most of the musicians I've met aren't exactly stranded on a desert island!

I am convinced my worst problem is me, not the devil whom I can resist, rebuke, and to whom I can quote Scripture until he flees (Luke 10:19, James 4:7). My worst problem is not the church that meets down the block that doesn't know what to think of (or do with) me. No. I am my own worst enemy . . . and you must realize it is exactly the same for you! The ultimate reason Christians are divided today is not lack of understanding or disputes over biblical issues. The bottom line is the lack of true love one for another. It is expensive! It hurts! You may have to dress way more conservatively than you'd like to in order to be really welcomed into a particular fellowship. Whether or not this is immaturity on their part or simply their stylistic preference showing, why add your immaturity to theirs? "Love covers over a multitude of sins" (1 Pet. 4:8).

In chapter one I related how essential a heart after God is. I mentioned that Bible study was one of the major points of fellowship and communion with Him. It should also be a normal part of communion between you and other believers. I found when my knowledge and personal practice of the Word became more important to me than my musical knowledge or awareness of the latest album by whoever, I had a lot more to fellowship with all Christians about. Before that, music and a very shallow understanding of my salvation with an actual ignorance of the Bible and its truth was all I had to discuss with anyone! Is it any wonder so many Christian artists' lyrics are without depth? Jesus said, "Out of the overflow of his heart his mouth speaks" (Luke 6:45).

Prejudice plays a major part in all of these matters as well. Start tearing down the wall of sin on your side. For those of you who are a bit younger, Paul's excellent advice to Timothy sums a lot of this up: "Don't let anyone look down on you because you are young, but set an example for the believers in speech, in life, in love, in faith and in purity" (1 Tim. 4:12). Many of us in the Church are waiting for you to join in with us so we can help you—and you, us—to grow in Jesus and share His love together. We're out here, honest. Maybe you haven't been looking. You can find us in most every denominational, inter- or nondenominational, Pentecostal, evangelical, Protestant or Catholic church. And though many Christians will beg to differ with this last statement, God will be the one who will alone judge the truth of it. For on that Day spoken of in Hebrews 10:25, there will be many surprises, I'm sure.

Again and again in Scripture, the Lord does what He does through the Church. Examine the following references for further proof of this:

> It was He who gave some to be apostles, some to be prophets, some to be evangelists, and some to be pastors and teachers, to prepare God's people for works of service, so that the body of Christ may be built up until we all reach unity in the faith and in the knowledge of the Son of God and become mature, attaining to the whole measure of the fullness of Christ.
>
> Then we will no longer be infants, tossed back and forth by the waves, and blown here and there by every wind of teaching and by the cunning and craftiness of men in their deceitful scheming. Instead, speaking the truth in love, we will in all things grow up into Him who is the Head, that is, Christ. From Him the whole body, joined and held together by every supporting ligament, grows and builds itself up in love, as each part does its work.

So I tell you this, and insist on it in the Lord, that you must no longer live as the Gentiles do, in the futility of their thinking. They are darkened in their understanding and separated from the life of God because of the ignorance that is in them due to the hardening of their hearts (Eph. 4:11–18; *see also* 1 Tim. 3:10, Acts 2:47, Col. 1:18–27, Eph. 5:25).

Many times in Scripture the Church is referred to as the "body of Christ." This is also quite relevant. The point is, we are His hands and feet. He is the Head. And His agency is the Church. One of the more interesting arguments in the Bible is discussed in Acts 15. It was a dispute regarding the Jewish rite of circumcision. The issue I wish to raise is that in a time of confusion, it was the local church that sent Paul and others to meet with the church leaders in Jerusalem in order to solve the dispute. And in Galatians 1:18–2:2, Paul speaks of submitting what he believed and had been preaching. Why? In order to be sure that he was doing the right thing. He was confirmed by those church leaders and thus continued his work.

One of my major concerns, during the past twenty-plus years I have been in full-time ministry, has been that too many pastors, evangelists, Bible teachers, radio/television ministries, and musicians have fallen into spiritual error or have in other ways sadly backslidden. One of the reasons? Because they have operated outside the covering of a local congregation/leadership situation. Many have held credentials with large denominations and were being used of God in many ways. But on a local, accountable, touchable, teachable, reachable level, the authority of others speaking directly into their personal lives and having hands-on access to their ministries just did not exist.

I have had experience serving on boards as well as chatting with those who serve on them. It is a known fact that simply because it is legally necessary to have a board doesn't mean the pastor, evangelist, or whoever is at the "top" in a given ministry gives any more than lip service to the other board members. What happens to these powerful, charismatic personalities through whom the Holy Spirit may move mightily? They become a church unto themselves, a church within the church, answerable to nobody. Boards staffed with yes-men are about as much of a godly challenge to the spiritual weakness and pride of the "leader" in such a ministry as are groupies to a rock band!

May I say it plainly? To these men I exhort: do not criticize contemporary musicians for that which you do likewise. To the musicians who have never truly sought out a local fellowship to send them out with blessings and prayers—it is time to build biblical foundations. You need their prayers and their understanding of the Bible and its major teachings. Like it or not, you are called to be part of a local assembly of Christian believers from the moment you trust in the Lord Jesus Christ as your personal Savior.

Membership and levels of commitment to a specific church will vary from assembly to assembly, yet this is something every musician must prayerfully yield to. Let me also go on record here as one who believes we musicians, if anything, must be *more* accountable to the local church we're plugged into than others in the congregation. Why? We influence so many more people.

Though we can judge others in our fellowship for superficial relationships to leadership, remember this: "From everyone who has been given much, much will be demanded; and from the one who has been entrusted with much, much more will be asked" (Luke 12:48). The lack of accountability many artists demonstrate at the present is appalling. How can we ignore what the Word so clearly states? Ministries are validated biblically if and when they are submitted to, and are an extension of, a local church. New Testament patterns are the model. Nothing more and nothing less. Listen to Paul's statement: "for fear that I was running or had run my race in vain" (Gal. 2:2). How much is done to no good purpose?

Is it any wonder why so many ministries and individual believers get so far away from simple biblical guidelines and sound useful teaching and practice? Because they are not a functioning church unto themselves, they cannot meet their interior needs. Independent music ministries are as unscriptural as other independent outreaches. Webster's defines *independent* as "not subject to control by others." Read Hebrews 13:17 again and think hard about your current situation. It is time to repent and "link up." Plurality and mutual respect and submission within the body of Christ is of utmost importance for wisdom, balance, and safety.

I want to insert one bit of practical advice at this point. You have to demonstrate a certain amount of respect toward anyone you work with regardless of the job, ministry, or whatever. When providing music in a ministering situation, a humble servant's attitude will be the thing most necessary to establishing and maintaining a relationship with those you work with and for. Please read the last two sentences over again! You see, submission is simply a normal part of life. Not only is it essential to ministering in your home church, but also in working with other believers when you're out on the road. Frankly, you won't have a road to be out on for long if you don't learn these lessons. And why should you? You earn the right to serve.

If praise and worship-oriented music is your calling, what better place to express your devotion to Jesus and to inspire others to the same than in a church? Although I don't believe every musician is particularly gifted in this area, I do wish more rockers would also learn to express a genuine sense of worship at several levels of volume.

Expressing your devotion to Jesus in this way is a true witness to Christians who don't share your love for rock. On one hand, we have nothing to prove. On the other, the quieter traditional church needs to be loved and educated out of their prejudices as much as we do.

If your music tends lyrically towards teaching and depth, church can be a place to share it. Even more evangelistic content can be used when ministering to a congregation. Many faithful churchgoers have no real personal relationship with the Lord Jesus. In some ways, the traditional church is one of the largest mission fields available. Whether your music ministry is primarily inside the church or to those outside, you will need the strengthening and support of a strong church family. You will need pastoral guidance to keep healthy in theology and doctrine.

Lastly, the traditional church needs your zeal as much as you need its knowledge. God bless you as you obey him in a lasting commitment to a strong Bible-teaching church. He can't bless you half as much if you don't. And remember to have patience with those "traditional culture" folks. You must learn to love them. For loving the Church is one of God's commands.

The Church at Large

Therefore, as God's chosen people, holy and dearly loved, clothe yourselves with compassion, kindness, humility, gentleness and patience. Bear with each other and forgive whatever griev-ances you may have against one another. Forgive as the Lord forgave you. And over all these virtues put on love, which binds them all together in perfect unity.

Let the peace of Christ rule in your hearts, since as members of one body you were called to peace. And be thankful. Let the word of Christ dwell in you richly as you teach and admonish one another with all wisdom, and as you sing psalms, hymns and spiritual songs with gratitude in your hearts to God (Col. 3:12–16).

Thinking of a musician who ministers outside of his or her local church brings to mind working and interact-ing with other believers. They don't know you like your home church does. They may not accept or appreciate you like your own fellowship does. And so we need to ponder a different kind of relationship in this context: the musician and the larger body of Christ.

Jesus prayed that all of His followers "may be one" (John 17:20–23). In His love alone is such a thing even possible! But are we really as divided today as some think? Is the Church as totally fragmented as is common-ly stated? We certainly have a lot of different folds with-in the larger flock, but we all follow one Shepherd. Jesus spoke of this phenomenon in John 10:16: "I have other sheep that are not of this sheep pen. I must bring them also. They too will listen to my voice, and there shall be one flock and one shepherd." I personally believe that just as each individual has his or her own unique personality, understanding, and sense of direction, so does each congregation in the true body of Christ.

The church at large has much more in common than it has differences—unless we major on the minors! At that point the most important central issues of the Word become obscured, and our uniqueness and personal opinions and tastes take the form of a bigotry that is absolute sin before God. Ninety-nine percent of all true Christians believe in the same basic Bible doctrines. But when hairs are split . . . so are we—one from another.

Musicians must be careful not to promote and magnify their own peculiarities to the extent that they obscure the basic unity and likeness all Christians share. It's one thing if another believer doesn't personally like your looks, dress, or sound. It's quite another if we end up causing divisions due to our own insensitivity. We each have to work harder at lifting up Jesus and forgetting about our individual and musical distinctiveness. Always. And especially in the presence of a Christian who may be questioning basic maturity if not our very salvation. For example, my brother's spiritual needs far outweigh the importance of my current hair color! You can bet I'm going to be trying to direct the conversation toward content that I hope will build him up spiritually—and we both benefit by that kind of discussion.

One thing is certain. If you find yourself traveling around the country (or world), you will learn many lessons about the incredible diversity within the Church. What you do with these experiences and how much you really learn from them will directly affect your own spiritual sense of balance.

Over the years, I have had the pleasure of meeting true Christians in nearly every kind of denominational (large and small) and inter- or nondenominational church. REZ has traveled to about forty-eight of the fifty states, nearly every Canadian province, and many foreign countries. Do you know what? There are true Christians in all of them.

In the fifth chapter of Galatians a number of positive and negative things are mentioned. In the New International Version, verse twenty ends with two words that need to be considered. They are *dissensions* and *factions*. In the Greek, they mean "disunion, division, seditions" and "a party, disunion, heresy, sect," respectively. These are very sinful attitudes that can disease any Christian. Here and in other places, the Word of God condemns such attitudes and activity. If you or someone you know has this sickness, it is high time to get with the Great Physician and repent! Love and humble sense will cure it. Pride, ignorance, and lies cause it. Thinking yours is the best church, music ministry, or whatever is one of the chief symptoms of this plague.

The devil will always agree with you—of course you have the "deeper truth and higher light." We are talking sin and nothing but sin!

What a difference love makes! And experience. Romans 15:5–7 is another text that deals with Christian unity. Verse seven is one I find myself quoting more and more often these days. "Accept one another, then, just as Christ accepted you, in order to bring praise to God." Some translations render the last phrase: "for the glory of God." What glory do you give to the Lord by your acceptance of other Christians? We cannot expect to agree with all others in all things always. Still, there is a mature "agreeing to disagree" when it comes to the less weighty matters of the law. We need not, no, must not unchristianize each other simply because we don't agree over every jot and tittle of Scripture! The Bible consistently teaches the intrinsic spiritual unity of believers.

Now, a short digression that may help to clarify some of the problems we face in using contemporary styles: The children of Israel were clearly told not to assimilate the moral habits and religious practices of the pagan nations that surrounded them or to intermarry with these pagan tribes. By the time Jesus is on the scene, this directive has been translated into an actual prejudice against anything "Samaritan." Of course, Jesus Himself holds to the commands of God in relation to the original concerns of God involving separation from pagan morals and practices. But He uses the Samaritan as an example of a good neighbor. Why?

If the practices and results of all Samaritans in all cases were sinful and a stumbling block to the Jews, how could Jesus travel through Samaria, take water from the cup of a Samaritan woman, and, in fact, state that when the Holy Spirit came, He would move the disciples to preach the gospel "in Samaria"? Remember, the Jews had interpreted the command of God to mean they should have nothing to do with Samaritans nor anything to do with their culture. This alienation is precisely what is happening among Christians today in the area of music and other cultural forms. Music has become one of the major causes of both unity and division among true Christian brethren.

Today's contemporary Christian musicians are the new Samaritans. It's that simple. What is not simple is cultivating a forgiving and merciful attitude towards older (in years or spiritual maturity) believers who oppose modern forms of music as anathema. Worse yet, we as individuals have also become anathema to some of them. We have to overcome this evil with good. We must respond with biblical compassion and understanding even though we may never win them over to our position. "Love covers over a multitude of sins" (1 Pet. 4:18). We must do as the good Samaritan did and "silence the ignorant talk of foolish men" (1 Pet. 2:15) by a holy and loving example of life that denies the very allegations of wrongdoing they throw at us.

It is a sad fact of life that racial, socioeconomic, cultural, and spiritual bigotry are not the exclusive domain of the unbeliever. How I wish I could report something else about our spiritual family ... God knows! Jesus said, "you will not see me again until you say, 'Blessed is he who comes in the name of the Lord' " (Luke 13:35). Volumes have been and shall be written on the unity we must demonstrate.

Musicians, of all people, ought to be able to see through the sin of division due to prejudice. We constantly face it with regard to our music. How is it, then, that we do not identify the very same sin in ourselves?

If the Lord grants you a more "traveled" ministry, in time you will learn to give Him glory for His immense wisdom in creating many, many kinds of people and just as many kinds of fellowships, ministries, and missionary groups through which to reach every and any one. His gospel and the fullness of Bible truth, sound doctrine, and principles of Christian discipleship are for all! So are His death and resurrection which are central to our individual salvation and sense of wholeness.

Learn to appreciate as well as walk in this truth: those who follow Jesus Christ as Lord and Savior are "accepted in the Beloved." This wonderful phrase is found in Ephesians 1:6 (KJV). As a result of our individual relationships with the Lord Jesus Christ we are blessed children of the most high God. In the original Greek words used here, there is a sense of coming to an end, consummation, and fulfillment. As we come into deeper realization of His (the Beloved's) acceptance of each true believer—realizing our own personal acceptance—we begin to appreciate the all-encompassing love of our mutual heavenly Father, and, likewise, how really rich and vast our family is.

It is a rare occasion indeed, when REZ tours or I go somewhere to speak, that we don't bring something good back home. Some blessing received or lesson learned from the church, house group, or prayer meeting we visited. There are so many diversified fellowships of Christian believers throughout the world. They have been given different gifts and leadings of the Spirit and are working in varying depths of understanding and biblical maturity. I find this marvelous! It means that God is larger and even more complete than any one of us hopes to realize in this life! It is a sad state for the Christians who are deceived into believing their own local fellowship "has it all." How small their God indeed is if their local assembly is the "perfect church"!

The flawless church with the complete Christian doesn't exist. So you need not worry because you are already aware that if they did exist they'd never let you be a member!

One final word, as you travel be cautious about new and strange teachings. Continue to be diligent in your own personal Bible study and commitment to your local church. If you are as secure and settled in these as you ought to be, you can enjoy the Lord Jesus Christ as He visits you via His Spirit among His followers—wherever they are gathered together (Matt. 18:20)!

Chapter Four
Responsibility to Your Potential Family

Though I am free and belong to no man, I make myself a slave to everyone, to win as many as possible. To the Jews I became like a Jew, to win the Jews. To those under the law I became like one under the law (though I myself am not under the law), so as to win those under the law. To those not having the law I became like one not having the law (though I am not free from God's law but am under Christ's law), so as to win those not having the law. To the weak I became weak, to win the weak. I have become all things to all men so that by all possible means I might save some (1 Cor. 9:19–22).

It is a sad fact that many in ministry today find it difficult to become "all things to all men" in order to win some. Maybe we don't want to win some? Possibly we want to be the big shots, the "stars" in some kind of fifth-rate Gospel music firmament. Some equate large numbers of ticket sales with success. Others mistake numbers of souls who prayed as the mark of success. If there are major needs in the body of believers today, balance and practical common sense are surely two of them. Humility will help open us to both.

Jesus was as at home on the dusty back roads of Galilee as He was in the big downtown temples (Mark

6:1, 35, 56). His heart was equally drawn to the poor widow and the rich young ruler. God is simply no respecter of persons (Acts 10:34). And when He looks into the soul of someone and reaches out to meet that particular need, He does so out of the fullness of who He is. I lack. We lack. But in Christ each of us can learn to do what we can to meet a need in a given situation. Too many of us pass the buck with regard to our music ministry. We are so specialized that we have only the most narrow musical vocabulary through which to speak, or we are immature in our lyrics because we don't have enough of the Word of God in our minds and hearts from which to draw. The same holds true with our concepts of how to help an individual who shares a problem with us after a concert. Of course we are not all called or gifted in every area mentioned in Scripture. But that fact must not be used as a cover for our natural inclination to run away from the hard questions. Many musicians display a spiritual shallowness and irresponsibility that is just amazing. To say we love Jesus, His people, and those who are still lost while claiming we're just dumb, illiterate musicians ("So don't come to me for the answers!") just doesn't wash. Someone once answered God that way: "I don't know. . . . Am I my brother's keeper" (Gen. 4:9)?

A Christian musician asked me to give him input for their group. Since I didn't have time to chat at length and his schedule didn't offer another opportunity, I shared one simple bit of advice. I asked that each of the band members—first individually, then as a group—seriously ask themselves one question: are they doing what they're doing in music as service to God and man or as an exercise in self-indulgence? The answer to that question would tell them a lot about the needs of their band.

If there is a genuine sense of calling on the individual/group to do God and man service, then we will begin searching His Word for answers—certainly for general solutions to the problems our audience brings. I am not at all insisting a musician function as a pastor or teacher or Christian counselor. But I am calling for those who find themselves in a music career as believers to "put on compassion," not to simply strap on a guitar. Think: there are Scriptures and experiences you have had where the Lord helped you find healing and solutions to problems in your life. Since you are saved, you know how to lead someone else to the Lord. There are churches, Christian leaders, books, seminars, radio/TV shows, other para-church ministries that can more directly and more thoroughly help those you talk to. Is it too much to ask you to use your heart and mind in offering some practical guidance for those in need at your concerts? I think not.

I am not suggesting you should have *all* of the answers to the many hurts and struggles or deep theological debates that the audience or congregation may bring to you. But again I must point to the Bible and its powerful Truth. Maybe some of us are just plain lazy. Maybe we don't think to at least pray with the person. Maybe we can't remember the name of that great Christian inspirational book by Dr. Whomever. Maybe we forgot to give them our church's phone number so they can chat with someone who can counsel them towards biblical solutions. Maybe we don't know of a good church in that area where they can be further ministered to. Maybe we just don't care. Am I being too harsh, my brothers? But take heart. Everybody was young once. All of us start at the beginning.

Where do we begin in reaching unbelievers? Peter had to grow in sensitivity toward the Gentiles. Paul helped him along. So if we are going to talk about our "potential family," we are going to have to figure out who they are and how they can be reached with the message of life. There are those who are rather stunted in their ability to cross over culturally. If you find yourself in such a condition, I recommend prayer, Bible study, and a walk through somebody else's neighborhood. What do they think? How do they feel? What are they subjected to at home, work, and play? Do they have any unique problems or cultural peculiarities? Ask them about some of these things. How simple, but how radical.

Even if you may not be specifically called to evangelize via your music, remember there are people in eternal hell who this very moment wish they had known what they know now! If that sounds too strong consider Jesus' story of the rich man and Lazarus (Luke 16:19–31). We have a potential family out there. Taking our responsibility to them seriously can make the eternal difference. Please be sensitive to this as you write, arrange, and/or perform your music.

How are we to find our potential family? Can we generate enough respect to be taken seriously? Paul did. But then he didn't bow to a religious hierarchy whose sense of respect had to do with laws not found in the Law. Nor did he cheapen his message by dropping to the moral level of those he ministered to.

The gospel will forever be an offense because God says so.

> As it is written:
> "See, I lay in Zion a stone that causes
>   men to stumble
> and a rock that makes them fall,
> and the one who trusts in Him will never
>   be put to shame" (Rom. 9:33).
>
> Brothers, if I am still preaching circumcision, why am
> I still being persecuted? In that case the offense of the
> cross has been abolished (Gal. 5:11).

But if our delivery of biblical truth and principle isn't met with respect it may well be due to us and not the content of our message. The responsibility rests with us to be sensitive to the Holy Spirit.

It is so much easier to spew forth biblical profundities rather than listen to people and relate to them as human beings! And this lack of demonstrative care is something I see constantly in my own life.

In any case, if we will work and think through these things we will learn what God wants to teach us about reaching those yet unreached. Growth will surely result unless repentance is lacking—in which case we will know what to do.

There are a multitude of Scripture passages that relate to evangelizing the unbeliever, and any true student of the Book will find them easily. As you become familiar with the Word, you will also notice much being said and done in order to encourage spiritual growth for the Christian. It is not an either/or proposition. Both evangelism and spiritual growth are essential in our Christian world.

> But to each on of us grace has been given as Christ apportioned it. This is why it says:
> "When he ascended on high,
> he led the captives in his train
> and gave gifts to men."
> (What does "he ascended" mean except that he also descended to the lower, earthly regions? He who descended is the very one who ascended higher than all the heavens, in order to fill the whole universe.) It was he who gave some to be apostles, some to be prophets,

some to be evangelists, and some to be pastors and teachers, to prepare God's people for works of service, so that the body of Christ may be built up until we all reach unity in the faith and in the knowledge of the Son of God and become mature, attaining to the whole measure of the fullness of Christ.

Then we will no longer be infants, tossed back and forth by the waves, and blown here and there by every wind of teaching and by the cunning and craftiness of men in their deceitful scheming (Eph. 4:7–14; *see also* Matt. 28:19, 20; Mark 16:15).

Paul was able to do both evangelism and spiritual growth kinds of ministry as the need called for it. As we each grow, we may find God directing us more generally towards unbelievers in our lyrics and presentation, or He may direct us more towards the edifying of the saints with our musical abilities. There are many streams of lyricism or presentation, but for my purposes we will consider only these two larger pools in which most Christian musicians swim (as it were). Obviously, doing either calls for an understanding of what the Bible has to say not only about the callings of God but also about the various spiritual gifts in the life of each Christian.

I have heard several thorough teachings on the gifts of the Holy Spirit. Regardless of your (or my) favorite exposition on the gifts, there are a few points relevant to those varied gifts that I think most of us would agree on. These points are worth exploring in the light of the issue I want to discuss.

We know that the Holy Spirit moves about, giving His gifts "to each one, just as He determines" (1 Cor. 12:11). This being the case, He, and not we, decides what gifts to give us. Much depends on what gift or gifts the Holy Spirit has endowed us with. The church can't reject musicians because they don't have a certain gift.

For example, no matter how hard you try to be an evangelist, the Holy Spirit may truly have gifted you in the area of teaching. While these are both scriptural gifts of the Spirit, one will lead you more toward evangelistic content in your song lyrics. If God has gifted you in teaching, you will probably tend to deeper depths of expository lyricism. You will be more moved to do tunes that lyrically provide lessons for the Church.

Over and over again, we see the Holy Spirit blessing individuals with various gifts through which to meet needs of the Church. While there is no "gift of music" listed in the Word, there is biblical basis for music to be referred to as a skill, not a calling or a gift as such. Okay, we see musicians are skilled and demonstrate various gifts of the Spirit, which will determine content. Therefore we have a scriptural foundation for our thinking and activity in ministry.

On the other hand, we need to remember that individual Christian musicians have vastly differing philosophies about how to do music and how they view music ministry.

I have a Christian friend who wants people to be saved, plays in a band that truly ministers evangelistically, and sees enduring fruit. He rejoices in that, yet he finds himself blessed greatly in playing an instrument skillfully. Is he in the "flesh"? Is he arrogant?

Could be. And he'll admit that these are battles he fights—just like the rest of us. My friend has wrestled with the fact that he is at least as happy with a strong musical performance as he is with souls committed to Christ at that performance. While he and I agree that the first pales in importance when compared to the eternal importance of the second, I believe I understand his situation.

Firstly, I know him well enough that I think I understand his heart before the Lord. Secondly, I assured him that as long as he lives under the biblical demands of a minister of the gospel and puts no stumbling block in the way of the evangelist in the band, it isn't a problem.

The evangelist is sharing out of the gift the Lord has given him. He is anointed for that purpose. The skill of the other musician is the store out of which he is sharing with the audience. Both are free in Christ to be who and what God has made them.

I have come to this understanding only after years of Bible study, preaching, and, yes, judging others. I could never understand why some musicians demonstrated so little apparent concern for the souls of those in their audience. Of course, some are living "in the flesh" and don't care about the eternal destination of those for whom they play. But for others who know and love the Lord and His Word deeply, their attitude is based on gifts and anointings of the Spirit rather than sin on their part.

Which brings me to the next point.

Believing that God has placed him in a musical group, the evangelist will not only naturally share the gospel but must also work at becoming musically skillful. Likewise, the skilled Christian musician must learn to share evangelistically although it might not be from the stage during a concert.

May I take you one step further? Should not the evangelist also be open and able to minister simple biblically edifying truth to a congregation of Christians? Let's say he doesn't have a teaching gift. Finding the entire church filled with firmly born-again Christians, should he evangelize them?!! Should he leave or refuse to get up and minister to the people? I think not.

In REZ Band, we often find ourselves in situations where everything possible is done to insure that non-Christians will come to a given concert. We will get into the evening and realize that the vast majority of the audience is already saved. No problem! Christians need to be challenged and fed, discipled and led into closer contact with their Lord!

At other times we will be ministering in a church situation. Though the concert sponsor has planned the entire evening to be one promoting Christian growth, it may turn out that few of those present know Jesus in a saving way. Of course, we will share the gospel, for that is the appropriate need of the people.

We need to think and study further with regard to callings, gifts, and skill as we find them in the Word. First, in order to eliminate confusion in our own minds and, second, to help the rest of the body of Christ think more biblically with regard to music ministry. Of course these principles apply to nonmusical saints as well!

Things are not as simple as they seem. Jesus commanded us to "go into all the world and preach the good news to all creation" (Mark 16:15). Does this mean that every Christian must preach? And what of the musician, the plumber, the cook, the housewife, the legislator? Must the artist load each painting with religious symbolism in order to witness? What about the command to make disciples of all nations? "Therefore go and make disciples of all nations, baptizing them in the name of the Father and of the Son and of the Holy Spirit, and teaching them to obey everything I have commanded you. And surely I am with you always, to the very end of the age" (Matt. 28:19, 20). Does this mean I must travel to every country possible and engage in church planting or that as a tourist I must find someone in the Grand Canyon to lead into the "meat of the Word"? There are more questions than pat answers in the life of many musicians today. I admit I have been shaken by the Holy Spirit to more closely examine some of my own laws and traditions. Balance comes hard to lawyers!

Some of these questions I ask seriously, others somewhat jokingly. Some are answered by a close reading of the Scripture in context. You can talk to your pastor or youth leader and read a good Bible commentary and come away with many if not most of the basic answers. "Do your best to present yourself to God as one approved, a workman who does not need to be ashamed and who correctly handles the word of truth" (2 Tim. 2:15).

I fear that there is a multitude of Christian musicians out there who are basically more in love with their art than with their "Lord" and more committed to their own pursuit of happiness than to winning the lost or encouraging fellow Christians with their music. We are talking selfishness, plain and simple. Proverbs 11:30 says, "He who wins souls is wise."

Allow God to be the one to determine who will be your potential family, then serve them according to their need in their language. Do not presume to force-feed them "the usual" in the usual way simply because you've always done it that way or because it is the more convenient, comfortable way. Serving up Truth by rote will accomplish about as much in the listener's life as serving God by rote will accomplish spiritual growth in yours! Do what you do from the most sincere and concerned heart. And remember to listen also. First Peter 2:17 speaks of showing respect to everyone. Let us continually bear this in mind as we do our music.

Souls most certainly hang in the balance.

List of Scriptures

Genesis 4:9

Exodus 20:3

Psalms 127:3–5

Proverbs 10:12; 11:14; 11:30; 12:15; 13:10; 15:22; 20:18; 27:5, 6

Lamentations 3:24–27

Malachi 4:6

Matthew 11:29, 30; 18:20; 19:3–12; 28:19, 20

Mark 1:21; 6:1, 35, 36; 12:29, 30; 16:15

Luke 4:16; 6:45; 10:19; 12:48; 13:35; 16:19–31

John 6:38; 10:16; 15:8, 13; 17:20–23

Acts 1:4, 14; 2:1; 2:47; 4:31; 10:34; 15: 1-41

Romans 9:33; 15:5 - 7

I Corinthians 6:20; 7:23, 24; 7:32–35; 9:19, 22; 10:31; 11:33; 12:11; 13:9, 13

II Corinthians 12:9

Galatians 1:18–2:2; 5:11, 20; 6:2

Ephesians 1:6; 4:7–18; 5:21, 25; 6:1–4

Colossians 1:18–27; 3:12–16

I Timothy 4:12; 3:10

II Timothy 2:15

Hebrews 10:25; 12:2, 5–17; 13:7, 17

James 4:7

I Peter 1:3–9; 2:15, 17; 4:8, 12, 18; 5:5

I John 4:19